C000141849

WHARFEDALE

Keith Wood

First published in Great Britain in 2010

British Library Cataloguing-in-Publication Data
A CIP record for this title is available from the British Library

ISBN 978 1 906887 96 4

PiXZ Books
Halsgrove House, Ryelands Industrial Estate,
Bagley Road, Wellington, Somerset TA21 9PZ
Tel: 01823 653777
Fax: 01823 216796
email: sales@halsgrove.com

An imprint of Halstar Ltd, part of the Halsgrove group of companies
Information on all Halsgrove titles is available at: www.halsgrove.com

Printed and bound in China by Toppan Leefung Printing Ltd

Contents

How to use this book

Wharfedale is the longest of the main dales running through the Yorkshire Dales National Park and offers both easy and more challenging walking in magnificent surroundings. The River Wharfe rises in the Pennines around Oughtershaw and initially flows from west to east along Langstrothdale before turning south at Buckden to flow along Upper Wharfedale, past Kettlewell and down to Grassington. Just below Grassington the river crashes over Linton Falls before continuing on past Burnsall to surge through The Strid at Bolton Abbey. At Ilkley the river turns east again eventually flowing into the River Ouse near Selby.

This collection of walks is concentrated along Upper and Middle Wharfedale between Buckden and Bolton Abbey

where the market town of Grassington is the main settlement and tourist centre with a Yorkshire Dales National Park Information Centre.

The U shaped valley, formed during the last Ice Age, is characterised by the green fields and hay meadows which are a profusion of colour in the early summer, enclosed by drystone walls containing a vast array of field barns. The village of Kettlewell is overlooked by the high fells of Buckden Pike and Great Whernside.

North of Grassington the traditional limestone scenery of the dales is well displayed with the dramatic cliffs of Kilnsey Crags opposite the limestone pavements above Conistone. The limestone gorge of Conistone Dib was formed at the end of the last Ice Age

around 15,000 years ago, when the meltwater formed a waterfall and cut back the soft limestone. Further up the dale further stretches of limestone scar are exposed above Kettlewell and Hubberholme – all are visited on walks in the book.

Each route is graded from Easy to More Challenging with further details of distance, height ascended and the type of terrain covered, to help with decisions of which walk to choose. The information blocks have distances and height gained in both imperial and metric measures, whereas in the body of the text I have kept to the old imperial units which still feel more appropriate (and comfortable) when describing the walks.

The walks are covered by the Ordnance Survey Explorer Maps OL:10 Yorkshire Dales Southern Area and OL: 30 Yorkshire Dales, Northern and Central areas. The maps in this book are only an outline version of each walk and the detail provided by the OS maps puts each route in context.

Every year tens of thousands of visitors enjoy the dales with the vast majority coming to no harm. However there are a few cases each year where walkers are injured, get lost or find themselves in some other kind difficulty requiring the assistance of the Rescue Services. A few simple precautions should help avoid any problems:

■ If you are unsure about your fitness start with the walks graded Easy and work your way up to More Challenging.
■ Wear suitable footwear – properly fitted walking boots are recommended for all the walks.
■ Take suitable clothing; the weather in the Yorkshire Dales can change very quickly, take a waterproof and extra warm layers to wear.

■ Take plenty to eat and drink en route, dehydration and lack of nourishment can lead to fatigue and mistakes being made.
■ An outline map illustrates each walk but it is recommended that a complete map is taken.
■ Inform someone of your planned route and expected return time.
■ Check the weather forecast in advance and only take to the more challenging routes on clear days.
■ And finally keep to the paths and watch where you are putting your feet – most accidents are caused by careless slips!

St Mary's Conistone

Useful websites:

Yorkshire Dales National Park
www.yorkshiredales.org.uk

Yorkshire Dales Society
www.yds.org.uk

Yorkshire Dales Millennium Trust
www.ydmt.org

Out of Oblivion Yorkshire Dales Heritage and Archaeology
www.outofoblivion.org.uk

Yorkshire Dales Tourism
www.yorkshiredalesand harrogate.com

Traveldales – Public Transport Information
www.traveldales.org.uk

Keith Wood Photography
www.keithwoodphotography.co.uk

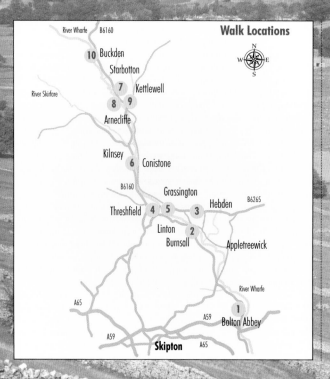

Walk Locations

River Wharfe B6160

10 Buckden

Starbotton

River Skirfare

7 Kettlewell

8 9

Arncliffe

Kilnsey

6 Conistone

B6160

Grassington

Threshfield 4 5 3 Hebden B6265

Linton 2

Burnsall

Appletreewick

River Wharfe

A65

A59

1

Bolton Abbey

A59

Skipton A65

Key to Symbols Used

Level of difficulty:

Easy

Moderate 🐾 🐾

More challenging 🐾 🐾 🐾

Map symbols:

🚗   Park & start

   Tarred Road

   Unpaved road

- - -   Footpath

■   Building

+   Church

▲   Triangulation pillar or other landmark

🚻   WC

🍴   Refreshments

🪣   Pub

1 Bolton Abbey and The Strid

A stroll through the Bolton Abbey estate up to Barden Tower and The Strid

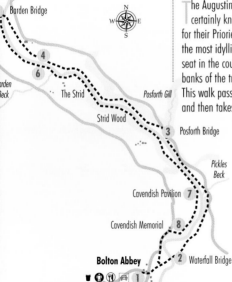

The Augustinian Order of monks certainly knew how to pick the sites for their Priories! This must be one of the most idyllic locations for a monastic seat in the country; situated on the banks of the tranquil River Wharfe. This walk passes by the Priory itself and then takes a circuitous route along the banks of the river, up to the medieval hunting lodge of Barden Tower before returning to pass by the impressive falls known as The Strid. Today the property is part of the

Level: 🖤 🖤
Length Miles and km: 6.85 miles (11km)
Ascent feet and m: Undulating 500 feet approx
Terrain: Dressed paths throughout
Park and Start: Bolton Abbey Estate car park
Start ref: GR 071 539
Info: Toilets at the start. Toilets and refreshments at the Cavendish Pavillion www.boltonabbey.com

Yorkshire estate of the Duke of Devonshire and is beautifully maintained throughout.

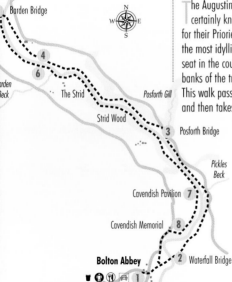

Barden Bridge

The Strid

Posforth Gill

Strid Wood

Posforth Bridge

Pickles Beck

Cavendish Pavilion

Cavendish Memorial

Bolton Abbey

Waterfall Bridge

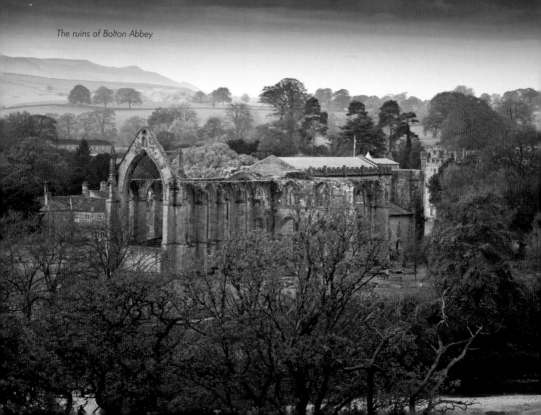
The ruins of Bolton Abbey

1 Leave the car park at Bolton Abbey, following the signs to the Priory Ruins onto the main road and walk a few yards along the road. Cross over and go through the "hole in the wall" to pick up a clear path past the ruined Priory buildings heading down towards the Wharfe.

2 There is a choice on how to cross over the Wharfe, either take the solid footbridge, or for the more adventurous try crossing the well laid stepping stones, formerly the right of way linking the hamlet of Storiths with the Priory. A fingerpost indicates the way showing "FP Barden Bridge 3¼ miles" to follow the route of the Dales Way upstream. Take the path up the hillside above the Wharfe to enter some woodland. Continue on

The Wharfe up from the Cavendish Pavilion

Bolton Abbey and The Strid

the high level path, before descending to cross Pickles Beck either through the ford or over the adjacent bridge. Immediately regain the path following the signs to Posforth Bridge and re-enter the estate through the stile or gate. Pass the Cavendish Pavilion on the opposite bank. Where the Wharfe splits just continue on the clear riverside path.

Footbridge over the Wharfe

 3 The path goes over a wooden footbridge adjacent to the stone built Posforth Bridge and the path continues upstream on the dressed path where the path enters the SSSI of Strid Wood. The path rises up to the shelter of Harrison's Ford Seat where the view opens out downstream along the Wharfe and the path starts to descend. Turning a corner one can see through the trees down onto The Strid below. Emerging from the wood the view opens out. There is a glimpse of the estate bridge and Barden Tower.

4 The path continues through pastures beside the Wharfe to reach a fine stone built Victorian arched aqueduct (bridge). If you don't fancy the extra stretch up to Barden Tower cross the bridge at this point and return from point 6. Alternatively continue on the right hand bank up to Barden Bridge.

Barden Bridge

Wood crossing over Barden Beck Bridge; keep left close to the river bank, passing the falls of High Strid and The Strid. Take great care if you choose to scramble down to observe The Strid. Keep to the main path on the right where the path forks to go to Ludd Stream Islands.

7 The path emerges from the wood at the Cavendish Pavilion, built in the 1890s as a tea room for the thousands of Victorian day visitors. Continue on the path hugging the banks of the Wharfe heading towards the Priory. Pass through the extended car park and leave the field through a wooden gate to cross another field and rise up the bank to meet the road at the Cavendish Memorial Fountain.

5 Upon arriving at Barden Bridge leave the estate for a moment and cross the Wharfe over the stone built bridge and immediately take the return path through the gate on the left. Climb the hill to visit the former hunting lodge of Barden Tower or simply start the return along the riverbank back to the arched aqueduct.

6 Arriving back at the four arched aqueduct pass through the smallest arch and continue on the path alongside the Wharfe. The path re-enters Strid

The ruins of Bolton Abbey

Bolton Abbey was founded in 1155 by the Augustinian order of monks, known as the Black Canons because of the colour of the robes that they wore. In the priory's heyday of the fourteenth century there were 26 canons and some 200 lay workers.

8 Take the path beside the road until it re-enters the Bolton Abbey estate. Follow the path down to the Priory to take a close look at the ruins and nave still functioning as the parish church. From here it is a simple matter of reversing the outward route back to the start.

The Strid

2 Burnsall and the Wharfe

A gentle stroll beside the Wharfe

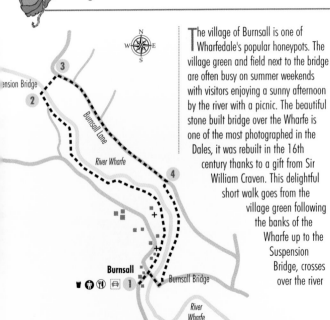

The village of Burnsall is one of Wharfedale's popular honeypots. The village green and field next to the bridge are often busy on summer weekends with visitors enjoying a sunny afternoon by the river with a picnic. The beautiful stone built bridge over the Wharfe is one of the most photographed in the Dales, it was rebuilt in the 16th century thanks to a gift from Sir William Craven. This delightful short walk goes from the village green following the banks of the Wharfe up to the Suspension Bridge, crosses over the river

Level:
Length Miles and km: 2 ½ miles (3.8km)
Ascent feet and m: 300 feet (90m)
Terrain: Riverside paths and a quiet lane
Park and Start: Burnsall Car Park
Start ref: GR 031 611
Info: Refreshments from the Red Lion Hotel and Wharfe View Tea Rooms at Burnsall

and returns along the quiet Burnsall Lane with views overlooking the village.

13

Burnsall Bridge

 Park in the small village car park just off the green beside the river in Burnsall. Start by walking towards The Red Lion Hotel to pick up the river bank path either beside the Red Lion or through the first arch of the bridge when the river is at a low level. The path is signed "Dales Way Path Hebdon Suspension Bridge 1 mile". Take the riverside path heading upstream along the tree lined banks of the Wharfe. The path passes around the back of Burnsall's church and follows the river as it meanders upstream. The path rises as the river sweeps around the exposed limestone of Wilfred Scar and the water tumbles over the exposed rocks. After the water rapids around the scars the river widens and the flow slows along a delightful stretch along the riverbank.

As the Suspension Bridge across the river comes into sight a narrow wooden footbridge crosses Sandbed Beck as it joins the Wharfe.

2 Cross over the Suspension Bridge or for the more

adventurous use the stepping stones over the river for the return along the opposite side. Immediately over the river go straight ahead on the gravel path. After just 20 yards along the path, go through the gate on the left and cross the back corner of a field to

Wilfred Scar on the Wharfe

topped Thorpe Fell Top. Burnsall quickly comes into view on the right.

4 At some trees a fingerpost points down to the right "FP Burnsall Bridge ½ mile" through a walled stile. The narrow path drops down through the woods before turning left and proceeding at a high level above the river. This narrow path above the Wharfe gives great views

a gate to emerge onto the surfaced Burnsall Lane.

3 Turn right to walk along the quiet single tracked Burnsall Lane for just over ½ mile. Cross over Mill Bridge and then follow the lane. The lane gently rises giving views across the valley to the heather-

Stepping stones over the Wharfe

Burnsall overlooked by Burnsall and Thorpe Fell

Burnsall's parish church is dedicated to St Wilfred. According to tradition, St Wilfrid visited Burnsall in the seventh century when he preached from a rock on the bank of the River Wharfe and baptised converts to Christianity. Wilfred founded the monasteries at Hexham and Ripon and became Bishop of York.

Burnsall Village

down onto the village of Burnsall. Leaving the trees behind the path drops down to the riverbank and crosses three fields on the way to Burnsall Bridge. Climb up the flight of steps onto the road across the bridge. All that remains is to turn right across the bridge and back to the start.

3 Hebden Gill and Grassington Moor

An exploration of Grassington's lead mining heritage

Grassington Moor was the centre of lead mining activity in Wharfedale. Records of mining date back to the fifteenth century when the monks of Fountains Abbey worked a smelt mill. Production peaked in the middle of the nineteenth century when upwards of 2,000 tons were produced. The mineral rights by this time were owned by the Duke of Devonshire whose principal seat of Chatsworth House in Derbyshire was largely paid for

Level: 🥾🥾
Length Miles and km: 4 ¾ miles (7.7km)
Ascent feet and m: 700 feet (210m)
Terrain: Gentle climb beside the beck, some road walking on the return
Park and Start: Roadside parking at Hebden
Start ref: GR 025 631
Info: Refreshments from the Clarendon Hotel in Hebden

by the lead mining profits – we have already explored more of his northern estates around Bolton Abbey in Walk 1. The walk gives ample opportunity to explore the industrial heritage around the top of Hebden Gill and across Grassington Moor.

Hebden 🚌 🍴 🏨

Scale Haw Falls

1 Start from Hebden where there is limited off road parking next to the Hebden Village Post Office and General Store. Begin by walking up the road on the left-hand bank of Hebden Beck. Leaving the back of the village the single track lane continues with a fingerpost "BW Yarnbury 2 miles". Walk along the single track lane gently rising up to Hole Bottom following the line of the beck. The beck tumbles over numerous minor cascades down on the right. It's worthwhile making the detour to visit Scale Haw Falls below the gritstone crag just off the road through a field on the right.

2 Reaching the lonely hamlet of Hole Bottom at the pair of gates take the right hand gate signed

Packhorse bridge over Hebden Beck

up the valley beside Hebden Beck overlooked by formations of millstone grit. Pass by the Hebden Gill Lanshaw Level intake which is opposite the Hebden Gill reservoir. The valley opens out as it passes the first signs of mining heritage with spoil heaps and abandoned buildings. Pass through the gate at the top end of the mine workings which proposes crossing to the left bank of the beck

"Public Bridleway Yarnbury 1 ½ miles No Unauthorised Vehicles". The unsurfaced lane crosses Hebden Beck over an ancient packhorse bridge and continues up the valley on the right hand bank of the beck. Pass the more recent Hebden River Flow Gauging Station and its weir. The ancient miners' track proceeds to gently rise

Ruined mine buildings

over a set of stepping stones in 100 yards. Cross over the beck using the stepping stones and continue heading upstream on the green path now on the left bank of the beck. Pass through a gate and continue upstream once again following in the steps of the lead miners of old. Where the track crosses over the beck continue on the left bank and rejoin the track in 100 yards when it crosses back again to the left bank and now rises through some spoil heaps.

3 The track drops back down to the beckside before almost immediately swinging around to the left away from the beck to head towards the disused Yarnbury Mines. Keep to the track as it zig zags its way up the hillside. Follow the main track through the gate in the wall signed "Bridleway" and continue to rise through the spoil heaps at Yarnbury. Looking over your right shoulder the cupola or smelt chimney can be seen on the horizon. Ignore the track joining from the left.

4 The track joins makes a T junction with the Duke's New Road, to continue on the main route turn left along the track to Yarnbury. Alternatively turn right for a detour to the chimney before returning to this

point. Now at the highest point of the walk follow the track to the buildings at Yarnbury. Pass by a row of sunken Bell Pits. There are various interpretation panels explaining the ruined workings on the Grassington Moor Lead Mining Trail.

Head of Hebden Gill

5 Arriving at the handful of buildings at Yarnbury turn left joining the surfaced road which heads down towards Grassington. Follow the single track road for nearly a mile across Grassington Moor down Moor Lane. Pass the isolated Mire House Farm on the left.

Edge Lane

Lime kiln beside Hebden Beck

6 Just as the road steepens down to Grassington passing Kent Furniture take the unsurfaced walled lane to the left signed "FP Hebden and Hebden Gill". The view now opens out looking down onto Grassington and along the valley to Skipton. Walk along the ancient Edge Lane with sweeping views to the south. Pass by a derelict farmhouse where the lane starts to rise towards a communications mast at the high point along the lane. Pass the Communications mast and the lane

Lead was not the only industry important to Hebden in the nineteenth century. Cotton production began in 1791 with the construction of a water powered cotton mill. During the mid nineteenth century production diversified to include worsted power loom weaving as well as mixed spinning, drawing and winding. The mill eventually ceased production in 1870.

now starts to descend and Hebden comes into view in the valley below.

 7 Go through a gate just above Garnshaw House where the

Garnshaw House

lane swings up to the left but keep straight on next to the wall heading towards Hebden. Past Garnshaw House go over the ladder stile over the wall towards a cottage at the far end of the next pasture. Go through a narrow gate stile signed "Footpath" pointing down towards Hebden. Cut across the corner of the next pasture to a ladder stile over the wall and go diagonally across the next large field to a narrow wall stile. Now keeping close to the wall go

over the ladder stile at the end of the next field and across the last large field aiming for the gate in the opposite corner. These last few fields act like sponges after heavy rain retaining the water. Leave through the gate at the bottom of field onto a narrow lane and following the "Footpath" signs walk back to the main road. The lane meets up with the main valley road at the Clarendon Hotel. Simply walk back down the road to the start.

4 Linton Falls and Thorpe

A suspension bridge, the Wharfe's best known falls and the villages of Thorpe and Linton

The ever popular Linton Falls just below Grassington are visited on this delightful walk together with the picturesque villages of Thorpe and Linton on the return. The route follows The Dales Way long distance trail beside the river down to the Hebden Suspension Bridge. Following the drowning of a local man crossing the river on the adjacent stepping stones in 1884, a committee was formed with the intention to build a footbridge. The new bridge was designed as a suspension bridge and was built by the village blacksmith, William Bell using 262 yards of redundant steel rope from the Hebden Moor Mining Company.

Level: 🥾 🥾
Length Miles and km: 5 miles (8km)
Ascent feet and m: 500 feet (150m)
Terrain: Clear paths and quiet country lanes
Park and Start: YDNP car park Grassington
Start ref: GR 002 637
Info: Refreshments from the Fountaine Inn, Linton

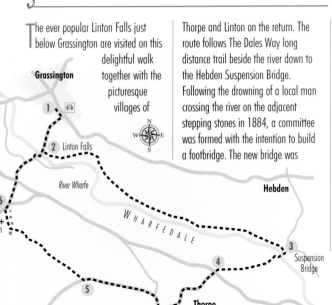

Grassington

1

2 Linton Falls

River Wharfe

6

Hebden

WHARFEDALE

3
Suspension Bridge

4

5

Thorpe

23

Fingerpost indicating the way from Linton Falls

Short cut over the stepping stones back to Linton

(1) Starting from the YDNP Car Park in Grassington walk down to Linton Falls along through the gate at the bottom left hand corner of the Car Park, signed "FP Linton Falls" down the narrow walled footpath.

(2) At the bottom of the path upon reaching the dramatic Linton Falls take the footpath on the left to Hebden and Burnsall just before the bridge over the Wharfe. This is the start of an easy stretch

through the meadows beside the river along the Dales Way. After passing through three fields the path emerges onto a surfaced lane over a wall stile; turn right and walk down the lane to pass a fish farm. Continue on the unsurfaced lane to reach a gate and follow the sign "Dales Way Burnsall 2½ miles" or for an ultra short

alternative cross the Wharfe over the stepping stones to return to the falls on the opposite bank passing Linton church. The gravelled path makes its way across pasture land cutting off a bend in the river past the water treatment works. The path re-joins the riverbank and follows along the tree-lined Wharfe all the way to the

Linton Falls

Suspension Bridge. It's a delightful easy riverbank stroll along this quiet section of the river. The suspension bridge and adjacent stepping stones shortly come into view.

 3 Cross the river using either

the bridge or stepping stones and follow the "Bridleway to Thorpe Lane" through a gate immediately on the opposite bank. The narrow path rises up the riverbank above the Wharfe. Go through another gate and continue straight on the faint green

path continuing to rise through the next field. A couple of waymarker posts assist in route finding to the gate at the top of the field where a "Bridleway" sign shows the way along the left hand edge of the next two fields. Arriving at the top of a

The Suspension Bridge across the Wharfe

Crossing the Suspension Bridge

rise through a gate there is just one more short field to arrive at a junction of roads.

(4) Take the minor road straight on continuing to rise, signed to Thorpe. This single track road continues to rise up the hillside. The lane loses height as it bends around the hamlet of Thorpe past the cream-fronted Manor House at Thorpe and collection of magnificent farm buildings. Continue along the

Thorpe Manor House

road as it swings back round to the right and rises up the other side of the village. Where the road forks take the left turn rising again along Thorpe Lane. The top of the hill is reached and the view opens out across to Grassington and up Wharfedale as the road starts to drop back down. Linton Church comes into view in the valley bottom.

(5) Don't be tempted by the walled path on the right signed "Bridleway B6160" keep on the road for another 100 yards and take the gated wall stile into the field on the right signed "FP Linton" and follow the green path down the left-hand side of the field heading towards Linton. The path passes the end of a tree plantation and straight

Linton Bridge

on down the next field to a farm gate through the opposite wall. At the end of the next field the path turns into a farm track which drops down towards Linton. Approaching a farm a trio of footpath signs point to the right; take

The impressive building beside the village green in Linton is the Fountaine Hospital. Bequeathed to the village as an almshouse for six local people by John Fountaine who made his fortune around the Great Fire of London. Built in 1721, the grand building and the adjacent chapel were designed by Sir John Vanbrugh.

the third one which goes along the edge of the field to Linton. Follow the footpath signs around the back of Grange Farm and turn right onto the road to walk through the centre of the pretty Dales village of Linton with its village green, pub and collection of crossings over Linton Beck; footbridge, ford, packhorse bridge and road bridge.

 6 At the road bridge turn right to leave the village along the

road which is signed "Linton Parish Church 12th C". At the crossroads go straight across with Linton Falls barely ¼ mile away. The road drops down with Captain Beck flowing through the fields on the left. At the bottom of the hill go straight on into Church Road which leads to the falls. Signs point to the footpath to the left to the falls. Cross the bridge back over the Wharfe and return up the narrow path into Grassington with the car park at the start.

5 **Grass Wood**

Walk through the historic Grass Wood Nature Reserve
returning along the banks of the Wharfe

Level:
Length Miles and km: 4 ¾ miles (7.7km)
Ascent feet and m: 600 feet (180m)
Terrain: Clear paths throughout
Park and Start: YDNP Car Park Grassington
Start ref: GR 002 637
Info: Toilets at start, refreshments in
Grassington

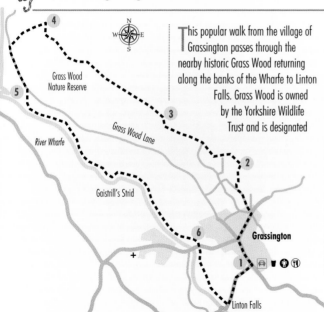

This popular walk from the village of Grassington passes through the nearby historic Grass Wood returning along the banks of the Wharfe to Linton Falls. Grass Wood is owned by the Yorkshire Wildlife Trust and is designated as a Site of Special Scientific Interest (SSSI). The wood supports a rich variety of wildlife and consists of ancient ash woodland over limestone scars. The wood also hides the remains of a number of historic sites including an Iron Age settlement and Far Gregory, a Brigantian Fort established to protect the native population against the Roman invasion.

29

Trio of barns leading to Grass Wood

1 Leave the YDNP car park in Grassington back onto the road and turn left to head towards the village centre. Turn right to walk up through the village square passing the Devonshire Hotel and then continue walking to the top end of the village past the Foresters Arms. Turn left down Chapel Street leading to Townhead. Pass Grassington's Methodist Church following the route of the Dales Way through the top end of the village. Approaching Bank Lane follow the sign "Dales Way Footpath to Kettlewell and Grass Wood Lane" up the lane to the right.

2 At a stables where the walled lane forks, take the metal gate on the left signed "Dales Way Footpath to Kettlewell and Grass Wood Lane" to begin to walk through the fields heading towards Grass Wood. Over a wall stile at the end of the first field a fingerpost points the way to the left "Public Footpath". Over a couple more wall stiles and at a muddy lane go straight across over another wall stile following the sign "Footpath to Grass Woods". Now follow the narrow but clear green path across the fields heading towards a collection of field barns on the way to Grass Wood. Crossing another stile the route enters an enclosed lane; take

It can get muddy!

the lane directly ahead passing by two well preserved field barns. At the end of the lane go through the right hand of the two gates following the "Footpath" sign through the next field heading to a third barn. Passing a mature ash tree and the third barn

The Wharfe beside Grass Wood

Walking through Grass Wood

the path swings to the right towards a wall stile at the entrance to Grass Wood.

 The path enters Yorkshire Wildlife Trust's Grass Wood

Nature Reserve where a clear path heads straight on through the trees. The path starts to gently rise through the woodland. At a slight clearing the path passes the site of a prehistoric settlement, and then continues to rise

Approaching Gaistrill's Strid

through the trees. Where the path forks take the path which continues to rise up to the right signed "FP". The path continues to rise through the wooded limestone valley with limestone scars to either side through the trees. Approaching the top of the wood the path levels off onto a dressed surface. At a crossroads of paths keep going straight on to "Grass Wood Lane" passing Fort Gregory on the left. Follow the wide dressed path which starts to descend through the wood heading to Grass Wood Lane.

(4) Approaching the end of the wood the track turns to the left heading towards the road. The wood changes in character approaching the road with beech trees and a clear woodland floor. Leave Grass Wood to join Grass Wood Lane; turn left to walk along the lane heading towards Grassington with the River Wharfe just across the fields to the right.

(5) Leave the road at a pair of metal gates to follow the Public Footpath back to Grassington Bridge. The path drops down through the trees to the riverbank and then follows the clear path along the riverbank towards Grassington.

Simply follow the delightful riverside path beside the Wharfe downstream. The path drops down to the river shore and then continues through the pastures around Grassington. The river gains speed and force as it goes through Gaistrill's Strid across some limestone rapids.

6 The arches of Grassington Bridge soon come into view and the path makes its way over the left hand side of the bridge up to the road. Cross the road and drop back down to the riverbank on the other side of the bridge to complete the riverside route down to Linton Falls.

The footbridge across Linton Falls is soon reached and all that remains is to turn left up the narrow walled lane back up to the car park.

The weir and adjacent derelict building just upstream from Linton Falls are actually the remains of a 1920s hydroelectric power system. The first power house on the site was built by the Grassington Electric Supply Company formed in 1909 to provide an electricity supply to the area.

Linton Falls

6 Conistone Dib

Walk up a dry valley to a unique geological feature

This may well be the shortest walk in the collection but it very much deserves its place, it's a walk into the real limestone country of the dales and is a geologist's and geographer's delight. Conistone Dib is a narrow gorge, which was created by post-glacial floodwater, and leads upwards through Gurling Trough to an area of spectacular limestone scenery. Walking up the drystream bed you easily make out where the water has carved its way through the soft limestone at the start of the walk. Emerging from the valley a section of limestone pavement is passed on the way to the unique pie-shaped limestone outcrop of Conistone Pie.

Level: ♥ ♥

Length Miles and km: 2 ¾ miles (4.4km)

Ascent feet and m: 600 feet (180m)

Terrain: Steady climb returning down a lane

Park and Start: Opposite the chapel in Conistone

Start ref: GR 981 674

Info: Refreshments from the Tennant Arms Kilnsey

35

Lower reaches of Conistone Dib

Upper reaches of Conistone Dib

(1) Start from the village of Conistone, parking opposite the old 1885 Weslyian Chapel now known as the Conistone Hostel where there is limited parking.

From the chapel walk towards the village centre and then take the unsurfaced lane heading out of the back of the village in the direction of Conistone Dib. Pass the Old Schoolhouse at the end of the village and go through the gate which is signed "FP Conistone Dib". A second fingerpost points the way "Public Footpath" into the confines of the dry limestone ravine of Conistone Dib. The route follows the course of an ancient riverbed with steep sided limestone walls. It's easy to imagine this would once have been a raging torrent as the route rises upwards through the twisting limestone walls. After the initial narrow section the valley widens and the route continues up the middle of the valley passing a number of enormous limestone cairns built from the vast limestone scree slopes on either side of the valley. As the valley opens out the path becomes short-cropped green turf as it approaches a gate through a wall with limestone crags ahead on the right. Pass through the kissing gate and continue on the

Limestone scars on the way to the Pie

Looking back down Conistone Dib

into a second high-sided and enclosed section of the valley. The now stony path again starts to rise more steeply with a drystone wall going straight up the middle of the ravine. The ravine narrows even more and nearing the top passes through a gate. One last climb

up a stone staircase which needs the odd hand for support the path emerges at the top of the ravine.

2 At a collection of walls initially go right through the kissing gate with a yellow waymarker and then

green path heading up the valley. Approaching the end of the walled enclosure another fingerpost points the way straight ahead up Conistone Dib through a kissing gate at the end of the enclosure for the route to continue

Conistone Pie

turn left to join the main track along the valley following the route of the Dales Way along to Conistone Pie. Go through a gate and follow the sign straight on "Dales Way FP Kettlewell" ignoring the bridleway to the left which will be used for the return to Conistone

a little later. It's well worth the minor detour to explore the magnificent section of limestone pavement which runs just above the Dales Way on the way to Conistone Pie which comes into view barely a couple of hundred yards along the wide green track.

3 A gated wall stile gives access to Conistone Pie. From the top of the limestone pie the view opens out up along Wharfedale and Littondale with the whalebacked ridge in between. The climbers' paradise of Kilnsey Crag across the valley completes the scene.

The view up Wharfedale from Conistone Pie

To return, initially retrace your steps back to the clear track near the top of Conistone Dib. Turn right and follow the track, known as Scot Gate Lane, downhill past the Wassa Hill radio communications mast all the way down to Conistone. As height is lost the view opens out across the valley to Kilnsey Crag. Nearing the valley bottom the now surfaced lane meanders down the hillside to arrive at the old valley road.

View down to the valley

(4) All that remains is to turn left and walk back along the old valley road back into the village passing the parish church of St Mary's Conistone.

St Mary's Conistone

7 Kettlewell to Arncliffe

Through "The Slit" and over Middlesmoor Pasture into the subsidiary valley of Littondale

Kettlewell is one of my favourite places in the Dales. Perfectly situated in the heart of Wharfedale on the route of The Dales Way, it is in the middle of some excellent walking country. You can spend a week in Kettlewell and enjoy a different walk every day and never set foot back in the car or public transport for that matter, such is it the hub of many different walks. This is the first of

Level: 🥾 🥾 🥾
Length Miles and km: 6 ¼ miles (10km)
Ascent feet and m: 1500 feet (455m)
Terrain: Two steady climbs and accompanying descents
Park and Start: YDNP car park in Kettlewell
Start ref: GR 967 722
Info: Toilets at start, refreshments in Kettlewell and Arncliffe

three walks in this collection starting from the village with its three pubs, various tea rooms and wide selection of visitor accommodation.

41

Leave the YDNP car park in Kettlewell and turn left to walk over the bridge over the Wharfe. Immediately turn right over the bridge and take the left hand track which rises up a track to go through a

The view up Wharfedale

"Through the wall stile"

gate which is signed "Bridlepath Moor and Footpath Arncliffe". Barely 50 yards through the gate take the path up to the left away from the track with a fingerpost pointing up to the limestone scar signed "FP Arncliffe" to what is known as "The Slit". The path gently rises across the first field, pops through a wall stile and then continues to rise more steeply. The path climbs steeply through the limestone scar needing the odd hand to ease you up and then brings you out onto the green

Looking back down onto Kettlewell

path continues to rise following the line of the wall on the left. The path unerringly rises over Middlemoor Pasture, joins a wider track for a while and then continues rising heading to another limestone outcrop

The Slit

velvet turf above the valley where a signpost helpfully points the way to the front right "Footpath". The path continues to climb steadily over Middlemoor Pasture. Ignore the track which heads off to the left; keep on the steadily-rising green footpath with ever improving views along Upper Wharfedale. Swinging round to the left the path meets a drystone wall, cross over the giant ladder stile and pause to take one last view down onto the village of Kettlewell overlooked by Great Whernside. The

which runs along the top of the ridge. Clamber through the limestone scar and the wall which runs along the top of the ridge is in sight 100 yards ahead with a ladder stile.

(2) Cross the ladder stile and continue on the green path which now starts to descend into Littondale. After a mile and 900 feet of ascent it's downhill all the way crossing the open moorland of the upper slopes of Old Cote Little Moor into Arncliffe. The path is occasionally wet in places on either side of the watershed.

Crossing the heather-covered moorland the village of Arncliffe comes into sight below and the path levels off for a while before gently swinging to the left to continue the descent to the alley floor. The path drops down below the limestone scar above Arncliffe to a wall to enter Park Scar Wood and then steeply descends the dry ravine through the wood to the village. Leaving the trees the path crosses two fields to emerge at the valley road adjacent to the River Skirfare. Go straight across the road and follow the footpath around the bend in the river to arrive at the village road.

(3) Turn left to cross the bridge over the river and follow the road round past the village stocks and the

entrance to the church. Leave the road and take the unsurfaced lane around the church which is signed "FP Hawkswick" to continue the journey, or alternatively take the opportunity to seek refreshment in the village. Follow the path around the back of The Vicarage Cottage to pick up the riverside path marked by yellow waymarkers to continue the walk heading downstream beside the River Skirfare. The path leaves the riverbank to cut across the fields. Just keep following the "Public Footpath" signs through countless stiles and gates dividing the fields heading down the valley. Approaching Hawkswick the path rejoins the banks of the river and arrives at a narrow walled lane and metal footbridge across the river. Cross the river using

Fingerpost across the moor

Arncliffe

opening out along Wharfedale at the end of Littondale. The path starts to rise again as it makes its way to the nose of the ridge between the two dales. Ignore the twin tracks coming down from the left, continue along the path gently rising up the hillside.

Littondale is rich in Bronze Age and Iron Age settlements. Saxon cultivation terraces (lynchets) can be seen in the valley. After the Conquest, the Normans turned it into a hunting chase before the land was granted to the monks of Fountains Abbey in the thirteenth century, and became extensively used for sheep farming.

the footbridge and turn right to walk along the narrow road into the hamlet of Hawkswick.

(4) Half way through the village past Bramblewood Cottage a fingerpost points up to the left signed "FP Kettlewell 2 miles". The unsurfaced lane heads out the back of the cottages through a gate and then up a walled lane leading back up the hillside. After an initial pull up the side the path levels off and continues along the valley with the view

5 Approaching the nose of the ridge at a limestone cairn the path splits – both end up at the same point. Either go immediately up the hillside to the left or go straight on and around the front of the ridge to arrive at the large ladder stile over the drystone wall which runs along the spine of the ridge. Cross over the wall and the path immediately forks; again both routes end up at the same place; I chose the slightly lower right fork which heads back up Wharfedale. Kettlewell comes back into view in the valley bottom. The path continues at a high level and passes two enormous limestone cairns at a section of limestone scree before veering off to the right heading back down the hillside heading towards Kettlewell. At a second limestone scar the path dives down again to a stile over a wall and then to another wall which skirts around a stand of trees, and continues its steep descent towards the valley bottom. Pass by an ancient ruined farmstead and go through the gate at the end of a paddock to pass into the light woodland along the valley sides. The path descends to meet the main valley road below; finally turn left and follow the path just above the road to the bridge over the Wharfe and back to the start point.

The bridge across the Skirfare

8 Starbotton via Moor End

Grandstand views of Upper Wharfedale from high above the valley side

Running between the villages of Kettlewell and Starbotton there are two high level and two low level routes on either side of the dale. These next two walks use all four routes. This first uses the high level path up the western side of the valley and returns using the low level path along the eastern valley side. On the outbound journey the buildings of Moor End are passed. These were first built for the manager of the nearby leadmines in the early eighteenth century. The Moor End mines were heavily worked between 1731 and 1879. Moor End was later used as a farm house until the 1930s.

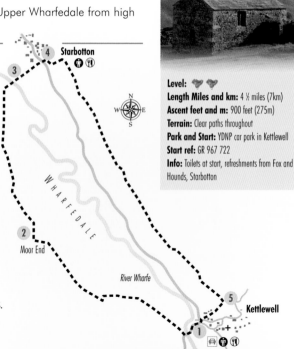

Level: 🖤 🖤
Length Miles and km: 4 ½ miles (7km)
Ascent feet and m: 900 feet (275m)
Terrain: Clear paths throughout
Park and Start: YDNP car park in Kettlewell
Start ref: GR 967 722
Info: Toilets at start, refreshments from Fox and Hounds, Starbotton

Kettlewell from the ascent

in front of a pair of gates; go through the upper gate and continue on the track which now starts to rise up the fellside in zig zags to Moor End. The track steadily rises up the fellside giving outstanding views along Upper Wharfedale to Starbotton and Buckden Pike with the patchwork of fields and barns decorating the valley bottom. After quite a climb the track levels off with the Wharfe meandering along the valley bottom below.

① Start from the YDNP car park in Kettlewell. Leave the car park and turn right to walk over the bridge over the Wharfe. Immediately over the bridge take the track to the right and then take the left hand of the two tracks which rises to a gate signed "Bridlepath Moor End and Footpath Arncliffe". Simply follow the rough stony track which heads up the valley, through a gate onto the National Trust's Upper Wharfedale Estate. Keep following the rough track. The track swings up to the left

Looking up Wharfedale

Shortly the lonely buildings of Moor End come into sight just ahead.

(2) Go through the gate into the Moor End yard, and then walk around the back of the buildings following the "Bridlepath" sign. Walk through an enclosure beside a wall to a metal gate at the top end. Go through the gate and keep to the path next to the wall following the "Bridlepath" signs to go through a

Barn at Moor End

Moor End

gap in a wall and now on a faint but clear green path the way goes across the upper pastures heading towards the village of Starbotton nestling beneath Buckden Pike. Keep following the Bridlepath signs through the high level fields. Approaching Starbotton

the path forks. Take the right hand fork which immediately starts to descend to a walkers gate through a wall where a sign reassuringly points "BW Starbotton". The path starts to drop down through the woods with the footbridge across the Wharfe just visible below. The stony path drops down through the trees. Leaving the wood behind continue on the path beside a wall heading down to the the river. Finally walk along a narrow walled lane which brings you to the footbridge across the Wharfe.

Every august since 1994 the village of Kettlewell has been taken over by a population of scarecrows. The annual Kettlewell Scarecrow Festival has become a major event attracting thousands of visitors to see over a hundred scarecrows situated throughout the village with both contemporary and traditional themes.

③ Cross the bridge and continue along the narrow walled lane on the opposite bank to join the main valley road at the edge of the village of Starbotton. For those in need of refreshment turn left where Starbotton's Fox and

The Wharfe meanders along the valley

Hounds will be found in a hundred yards or so.

④ To continue the walk go straight across the road and immediately behind the first cottage in the village a fingerpost directs you

Starbotton overlooked by Buckden Pike

to "Kettlewell 2 miles" through a gate to enter the pastures for the return down the valley. The path gently rises through the first three fields before climbing a high step stile at the end of the third enclosure. The path turns to the right to make its way back along the valley. with Moor End in sight high on the opposite side of the valley. The grass path makes its way along the valley through countless fields on its way back to Kettlewell. The path soon draws level with Moor End on the opposite side of the valley. Climbing a wallstile the route passes through the newly planted Cross Wood. After crossing over numerous stiles the buildings of Kettlewell come into sight with the whitewashed building of the Racehorses Hotel being particularly prominent. There is

an excellent view across the valley to the ridge, limestone scars and The Slit crossed over in Walk 7.

5 Approaching Kettlewell the path swings down to the right and heads down a narrow walled

lane to emerge at the back of the village just along from the Youth Hostel and Post Office. All that remains is to keep walking straight on which brings you onto the main valley road next to the two village inns and back to the start.

The Wharfe from the footbridge

9 **Starbotton over Cam Head**

Classic walk from Kettlewell over the top to Starbotton

This is the third walk from Kettlewell and utilises the remaining two routes up the valley between Kettlewell and Starbotton. This route takes the high level pull up the eastern side of the dale to Cam Head for the outward journey, returning in more gentle fashion along the Dales Way besides the banks of the Wharfe on the western side of the valley. This walk is a particular favourite of mine, especially

Level: 🐾 🐾 🐾
Length Miles and km: 6 miles (9.75km)
Ascent feet and m: 1100 feet (330m)
Terrain: Long steady pull uphill, sharp descent returning along the valley bottom
Park and Start: YDNP car park in Kettlewell
Start ref: GR 967 722
Info: Toilets at start, refreshments from Fox and Hounds Starbotton

as it's an excuse to stop for a pint at the Fox and Hounds. So save this one for the middle of the day to be able to have lunch halfway at the pub!

Cam Head

Starbotton Cam Road

Starbotton

River Wharfe

Top Mere Road

W H A R F E D A L E

Kettlewell

1 Leave the car park and turn left towards the village; cross the bridge over the beck in front of the Racehorses Hotel. Turn right immediately over the bridge in front of the Bluebell Inn and with the beck now on the right go up the lane through the village passing by the Village Hall on the left. At the end of the lane go straight over the crossroads at the Village Store and

Blue skies above Starbotton Road

continue walking up through the village.

2 At the top of the village the road swings around to the left following the sign to Leyburn indicating a gradient of 1 in 4 and immediately starts to climb. About 100 yards up the road, the road

bears around to the right and an unsurfaced drover's road enclosed between two drystone walls goes straight on. This is the "Top Mere Road" up to Cam Head sign-posted "Bridleway to Starbotton 3 ½ miles" that you are going to follow. The track rises steadily with delightful views along Wharfedale with its

Kettlewell from Top Mere Road

patchwork of drystone walls and dales barns to the front left. The views get increasingly better as height is gained but don't miss the opportunity (pausing for breath) to look behind to enjoy the views down the dale to the south.

Eventually the lane levels off and reaching open moorland panoramic views open up to the right across to Great Whernside. Listen out for the

calls of curlew, lapwing and the song of the skylark whilst crossing the open fell on the top of Cam Head. Hold your nerve as you walk along the clear path across Cam Head which safely delivers you to a clear junction with a fingerpost.

3 Upon reaching the junction with Starbotton Road marked with a finger post, turn sharp left almost back on yourself towards Starbotton. After a stretch of level walking passing through two walls, enter the walled track of Starbotton

Fox and Hounds, Starbotton

Wharfedale from Top Mere Road

Footbridge over the Wharfe

Cam Road to commence the steep and winding descent to the valley bottom and the village. As you lose height, Wharfedale comes back into view with its drystone-wall-enclosed pastures and Buckden Pike is seen to the front right. Nearing the bottom of the road just before reaching a gate, Starbotton can be seen below over the wall to the left. Pass through a gate and continue down the lane to the village. Just before the cottages the lane gains a concrete surface and through a gate you enter the pretty little dales village of Starbotton. Walk through the back of the village down to the main road.

4 To continue the walk turn left along the main road in front of the traditional red phone box, or for those in need of a break turn right to have a pint at the local pub the Fox and Hounds. Having gone left at the phone box, go along the road for 100 yards and take the narrow lane to the right signed "Bridleway to Arncliffe" and "Footpath Kettlewell 2 miles". Walk down the narrow lane heading towards the river.

Fingerpost across the moor

BW ARNCLIFFE 2¼
FP KETTLEWELL 2
FP BUCKDEN 2¼

5 Cross the narrow footbridge over the Wharfe and turn left at the other side. Follow the footpath sign to Kettlewell having passed through a wall stile. Now follow the route of the Dales Way along the banks of the river heading back to Kettlewell. Keep following the finger posts through a series of pastures crossing through numerous gates and over some enormous ladder styles. Enjoy the gentle return along the valley bottom through the delightful typical dales scenery on springy turf paths through fields dotted with barns. As the path draws level with the village school across the river, the path passes through a small wood and drawing close to the village the sound of passing cars on the nearby road begins to be heard.

6 Opposite the car park pass through the last gate to walk the remaining few yards next to the river up to the bridge. Pass through a gate to join the main road and turn left to cross the bridge back over the river and to the car park beyond. As you cross the bridge you can see the outward route of the Top Mere Road going up the fellside.

The village of Starbotton was inundated by a major flood in 1686. Rain is said to have descended with great violence for an hour and a half high on Buckden Pike followed by a raging torrent down Cam Gill Beck destroying a third of the village and leaving the villagers to flee for their lives.

The Yorkshire Savanna!

10 **Cray and Hubberholme**

A triangular exploration around the three settlements at the head of Wharfedale.

This popular walk around the head of Wharfedale before it turns west and becomes known as Langstrothdale visits the three settlements of Buckden, Cray and Hubberholme. Walkers in need of refreshment are well served with pubs in all three hamlets. Reaching a height just short of 1200 feet (360m) at a cairn high above the valley a full length view along the

valley presents itself. The route passes by the historic Scar House above

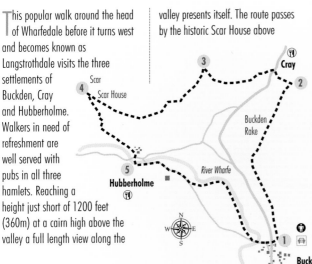

Level: 🐾 🐾
Length Miles and km: 5 miles (8km)
Ascent feet and m: 700 feet (210m)
Terrain: Steady climb from the start then easy walking on clear paths
Park and Start: YDNP car park at Buckden
Start ref: GR 941 772
Info: Toilets at start, refreshments at Cray, Hubberholme and Buckden

Hubberholme. George Fox, the founder of the Society of Friends or Quakers visited Scar House on his transforming journey from Pendle Hill in 1652.

Looking down onto Hubberholme

(1) Leave the YDNP car park in Buckden through the pair of gates at the far top corner of the car park to join a clear track heading up the hillside. The track passes through the National Trust's Upper Wharfedale Estate and is signed "Public Bridleway

View from Buckden Rake

Track through Rakes Wood

Buckden Pike and Cray High Bridge". The clear track immediately starts to gently rise up the lower slopes of Buckden Pike looking down onto the patchwork of fields laid out in the valley bottom. The steadily rising track

passes along the edge of Rakes Wood. Leaving the trees behind the path continues to rise and swings around to the right around Buckden Pike. As the track levels off it forks; take the left hand fork which goes straight on.

View from the cairn

Continue straight on until a walkers' gate through the wall on the left comes into sight signed "FP Cray".

(2) Go through the gate and descend on the path through the fields to the hamlet of Cray. The path emerges through a wooden gate to cross over Cray Gill either across the ford or over the stepping stones to arrive at the main road and the

Proceed through a gate into a large walled enclosure where a "Footpath" sign confirms the direction to Cray High Bridge. The green path known as Buckden Rake crosses the field to a gate ahead at the far side. The view

opens out to the limestone scars and an impressive barn in the meadows on the opposite side of the valley. Pass through the gate and continue along the level with the hamlet of Cray appearing down to the left.

Hay meadows near Cray

White Lion Inn at Cray. Cross the road and continue on the track around the back of the pub signed: "FP Stubbing Bridge and Yockenthwaite". Further round the back of the pub follow the track up to the right signed "Footpath". Pass around the back of some farm buildings where the clear track continues on the level around the back of Cray; shortly another Fingerpost confirms the direction. A further gate leads into the pastures with a sign "FP Scar House and Yockenthwaite". The clear path heads through the hay meadows to pass by the impressive field barn where a fingerpost indicates the direction ahead to a narrow wooden footbridge over Crook Gill at the top of a wooded ravine.

3   Cross the footbridge and continue on the wide green path between the trees and limestone scars. Just ahead to the front right a stone cairn can be seen on a higher point. Continue along the path and at an appropriate point veer off to the right to visit the cairn. It's worthwhile making the detour to visit the cairn for a stunning full length view along Upper Wharfedale, down to Buckden with Kettlewell in the distance. From the cairn simply drop back down to rejoin the main path and keep heading west towards Scar House. Pass through a tall and narrow wall stile where the green path continues along the edge of the limestone scar towards the aptly named Scar House.

4   The trees around Scar House are reached and the path proceeds over exposed limestone scar. Around the back of the buildings a fingerpost points the way to Hubberholme through the buildings. A clear unsurfaced track makes its way down the hillside from Scar House towards the valley bottom and Hubberholme. Approaching the valley bottom the track levels off and

Hubberholme church

Hay meadows in Wharfedale

The church of St Michael and all Angels at Hubberholme has three claims to fame. It is noted for its magnificent sixteenth century rood loft. The oak pews were made by Robert "Mouseman" Thompson of Kilburn. Finally the church is the resting place of the ashes of the writer and playwright JB Priestly.

continues to Hubberholme. Finally the track drops down to pass the church of St Michael and All Angels, crosses the bridge over the Wharfe and

Dales Way Footpath Buckden Bridge ¾ ML

Fingerpost across the moor

meets up with the main valley road at the George Inn.

(5) Turn left onto the road for a short distance of unavoidable road walking. Take the usual care along the narrow road heading back to Buckden. After nearly half a mile a wide gate on the left leads through the fields signed "Footpath Only"

with Buckden Bridge now only ¾ of a mile away. The wide path proceeds along the edge of the fields following the route of the Dales Way. Joining the riverbank follow the path back to Buckden Bridge. Approaching Buckden the path emerges back onto the road; turn left to walk over the bridge and back up into the village and the start point.